I0486785

Common Sense Tax Reform

by

Duard Lawley

authorHOUSE™

1663 Liberty Drive, Suite 200
Bloomington, Indiana 47403
(800) 839-8640
www.AuthorHouse.com

First published by AuthorHouse 09/23/05

ISBN: 1-4208-8312-7 (sc)

Library of Congress Control Number: 2005908163

Printed in the United States of America
Bloomington, Indiana

This book is printed on acid-free paper.

Author's Background

Duard Lawley is a certified public accountant (Retired), a licensed CPA in the state of Idaho for forty-five years.

Duard opened his first tax preparation business in the filing season of 1950 when he was in his senior year of college at Northeastern State College, Tahlequah, Oklahoma. After graduating from college with a degree in Business Administration he entered the U.S. Navy in September 1950 and spent four years in the service, including service in the Korean War. During the years of service he was appointed tax consultant for his ship complement for two years and worked after hours in a public accounting office in Norfolk, VA.

After his Navy service, Duard moved to Colorado Springs, Colorado, and opened a bookkeeping and tax service. It was very successful but, the Air Force Academy boom did not suit his nature so the practice was sold and he moved to Twin Falls, Idaho in 1957.

After being engaged in life insurance sales for a period of time Duard returned to accounting and tax return preparation in 1959 and operated as a public accountant until qualifying for his CPA certificate in 1960. He was in practice as a sole practitioner until 1974, merging then with another firm in Carson City, Nevada in which he became co-senior partner. The firm became a regional practice with five offices in the states of Idaho, Nevada and California.

Duard retired from the firm in 1975 due to health problems and spent the next few years as a part-time tax and business consultant and investor in real estate. He opened another small office in 1988 and operated it until 2004.

Acknowledgements

The idea of this book was born in 1992 and was wholeheartedly supported by my brother, Gene Lawley, BSc. MBA, CPA. , who was then, and has been since, one of my most vigorous supporters and has done yeoman work in helping with research and development.

Congressman Bill Archer 1971-2001, Chairman, House Ways and Means Committee in 1992 was a deciding factor in initiating this book at the beginning. His letter to my brother, Gene, outlining the required characteristics of an eminently fair, broad-based tax system for the twenty-first century, opened my eyes to the requirements of the taxpayers of America. That letter is reproduced later in the book.

Senator Larry Craig, Idaho, who has supported our efforts since the beginning and who has consistently advanced the idea of a broad-based consumption tax system.

Senator Mike Crapo, Idaho, also a longtime supporter of the consumption tax system.

Past Senator from Idaho and now Governor of Idaho, Dirk Kempthorne, has also backed a change in the tax system.

Ron Hardy, Ph.d. Director of Aquaculture Research, University of Idaho, a loyal friend and contributor of both technical and theoretical ideas.

Don Ballew, DDS(Ret.), Elk City, Oklahoma, life-long friend and supporter, for wonderful insight and both technical and ideological advice and enthusiasm.

Pat Parrott, Anita Parrot and a number of other long-time clients and friends contributed invaluable advice and support. Thank you.

Foreword

America, wake up! And soon! Otherwise, we are doomed in our battle to sustain the American dream. There are enemies within and they are on the attack. They are attacking our morals, our vision of the quality of life, and our time-honored love of life, liberty and the pursuit of happiness. And one of the weapons they are using and have been using for almost a century is that insidious but supposedly necessary fixture, the graduated income tax.

The graduated income tax didn't really come into play as a device of re-distribution of wealth until after World War II. It had been in force for a number years but didn't sound like a bad idea to most of America during the depression years when most people were not affected by the tax, only the wealthy. It had been used as a weapon against criminals such as Al Capone but was not a force in the lives of the average family.

In the fifty-odd years since World War II, however, the graduated income tax has become the master plank in the platform of the Liberal/Socialists who desperately desire the transformation of America into George Orwell's world of *1984.* The insidious worm is now so imbedded in American consciousness that almost no one ever imagines that they could possibly get a paycheck without that inevitable "Federal Withholding Tax" deduction on it.

The graduated income tax is a perfect tool for Socialism in all its disguised forms. As a tool for re-distribution of wealth, it, along with an estate (death) tax reduces initiative and restricts savings. Worst of all, personal and financial privacy, a basic tenet of freedom, is also restricted, almost to the point of invisibility.

In the writing of this book a number of questions came to mind and I wondered why they haven't impinged on the minds of taxpayers in a more prominent way over the years. I have prepared or overseen thousands of tax returns and few people have seemingly ever raised the obvious question, "Why?" I suppose they trust the American way and assume that a graduated income tax has been around a long time and must be part of the American dream.

Actually, the tax has been around a long time but has never been questioned, mainly because the backers have enticingly played upon the greed (or ignorance) of voters who yearn for the "pie-in-the-sky" solutions promised. Many voters blindly follow leaders who have no solutions, only defamatory speeches and oratory.

I have endeavored to lay out a tax plan that will once again set us back on the right course to follow the American dream, a tax plan that will broaden the tax base, lower the rate of tax and put the tax on a pay-as-you-spend, rather than the horrible mess we have today. The Universal Transaction tax is a tax for the twenty-first century, not a carryover from the late nineteenth or early twentieth century. It is a tax easily understood and best of all, it is not collected by force and there are no returns to fill out.

I would like to introduce to you a tax based on common sense, not a tax of definition. I hope you agree with me after reading the book. Let's modernize and simplify our tax system. Save our America!

Table of Contents

Chapter One

It's Time to Kill the Graduated Income Tax

Our tax system is broken beyond repair. The "graduated income tax" has deteriorated in to such a mind-boggling mess it is ridiculous. How did we get into such a situation? If we don't extricate ourselves, and soon, we might lose our birthright of freedom.

The graduated income tax is a tax of definition, made to order for the "taxing" politicians and bureaucrats. "Income" can be one thing to one person or group and quite a different thing to another group. We have added a great number of words and phrases to normal use. Words like "adjusted gross income", "capital gains", "and capital losses", "depletion". The Tax Code is approaching fifteen thousand pages of small type and grows at a faster pace each year. We have truly reached very close to the bottom of the barrel when we came up with the "Alternative Minimum Tax". We have tax cuts that pop up in some other area as decreases in a prior tax credit.

Nothing is new in the statements above. Writers have written substantially the same things for years now. Interest in any different base of taxation grows yearly around April 15 as editors have to at least put something in their publication that the taxpayers will read.

I believe my credentials for making the above statements and, indeed, for the entire book, are certainly beyond reproach. I prepared my first income tax return in March of 1945. The filing deadline in those days was March 15 and it was very tough to get an extension. The return was for an uncle who had a little hard-scrabble farm down in the Cookson Hills of northeastern Oklahoma. As I recall, though, it was only a two-page return, even including the Schedule F. And, believe it or not, the Schedule F (for farmers) has hardly changed in format in the almost-sixty years since.

In those early days I seem to remember that there was a feeling that the system was fair, even though burdensome. That was during World War II, however, and it was considered for a good cause. People worried about filing on time, keeping current on their taxes and were somewhat proud of being able to pay taxes in a free economy and enjoy the protection of the Bill of Rights and the Constitution

Over the long period of years, many of those protective devices have been eroded by one pressure group or the other, each trying to worm its way into just a tiny bit more "equality" than the next.

Few people have personal or financial privacy now. I can purchase a computer disk with thousands of names on it that can let me pry into almost intimate details of the lives of thousands of individuals and families anywhere in the United States. I have received many questions from clients about the ability of the taxing authorities to conduct random searches of their bank accounts. This is supposed to be forbidden but many people believe it happens, anyhow.

Until about twenty years ago I knew of no one who was not filing income tax returns on a regular basis and it was real news when the IRS picked up someone for failure to file returns for several years. People seemed sure that the system was fair. Then, the government started using the income tax system for "social control" and the age of pressure groups began in earnest. We had tax incentives to "spur the economy", "promote savings", "protect minorities", "put the crooks out of business' and God knows what else floated through the Regulations unnoticed.

Today, I know of, just in my small circle of people and acquaintances, several people (and a couple of corporations) that have not filed returns for up to seven years. And they are relatively unconcerned about it. As one person told me once, "I don't think they would send me to jail because they wouldn't have room for all of us who are not filing." And, you know, he just might have been right.

As Willie Sutton, the bank robber, once said when asked why he kept robbing banks, "Well, that's where the money is." In any taxing system the same theory has to apply. I believe that over the past sixty-or-so years out taxing system has deteriorated to the extent that we are taxing the wrong areas. Why not "go where the money is?" And that heads us in the direction of the fairest and yet most liberal of all taxes consumption tax of the most basic sort, a tax on <u>cash</u> <u>flow</u>.

Chapter Two

The Universal Transaction Tax

The Universal Transaction Tax is a consumption tax that is reasonable and fair to all taxpayers, a one percent (1%) tax on the gross amount of all transactions made----no deductions, no exemptions, no massive regulatory definitive process, no army of auditors and collectors. This tax would affect every individual, every corporation, and every organization in the country. It would also affect foreign entities if they effected transactions in this country. Charitable entities would not be exempt. The tax would apply on all sales, wholesale and retail.

This all sounds good and extremely desirable and has been dreamed of before but would immediately be discarded by most people as being uncollectible and extremely cumbersome considering all the returns to be filed. It would, on the surface, seem so, but let's look a bit closer at the mechanics required. We are, at present, hip-deep in regulatory forms and filings. We have to deposit withheld payroll taxes in a Federal Reserve Bank almost as soon as they are withheld. Why not require all collectors of taxes (which would include almost all entities) to have a bank account. When they made their bank deposit they would also make the deposit of the collected tax. This is what almost all business entities are doing already.

When I showed this idea to one of my banker friends he looked over the proposal and immediately threw up his hands in horror and said, "No way! This will never work. We'd go broke taking care of the government's money." When I explained to him that the computers would take care of most of the work and that the bank would be paid a fee for every transaction recorded (they don't get anything now) he brightened considerably and said he thought it was a great idea.

The transaction tax could not have been even a remote possibility twenty years ago. Computer technology has brought us to the point where we can consider such a tax collection process. And the beauty of the system is that the government gains almost a full year of time. Instead of having to wait for over a year for some tax and having to refund over-payments they would get their tax within just a few days and there would be no refunds to worry about.

A windfall of monumental proportions would occur in the first year of a transaction tax implementation. All taxpayers would have to pay their prior year taxes on their final returns plus they would have been paying the transaction tax beginning on January 1 of the New Year. Fiscal year filers (mostly corporations) would have their normal two and one-half months to file and pay any taxes due. Conceivably, it could happen that a corporation with a fiscal year ending November 30 of the final tax year would pay their final tax on February 15 of year 2 of the transaction tax.

It would seem that this windfall could reduce the national debt or shore up the social security system or beef up health care reserves. What a battle would ensue if this ever happened!

One of the bright points of a transaction tax is that the government would get out of the collection business and let the people of America collect their own taxes the easy way--- at the cash register! The IRS would still be in business without the many thousands of employees they now have but with fewer taxpayer conflicts.

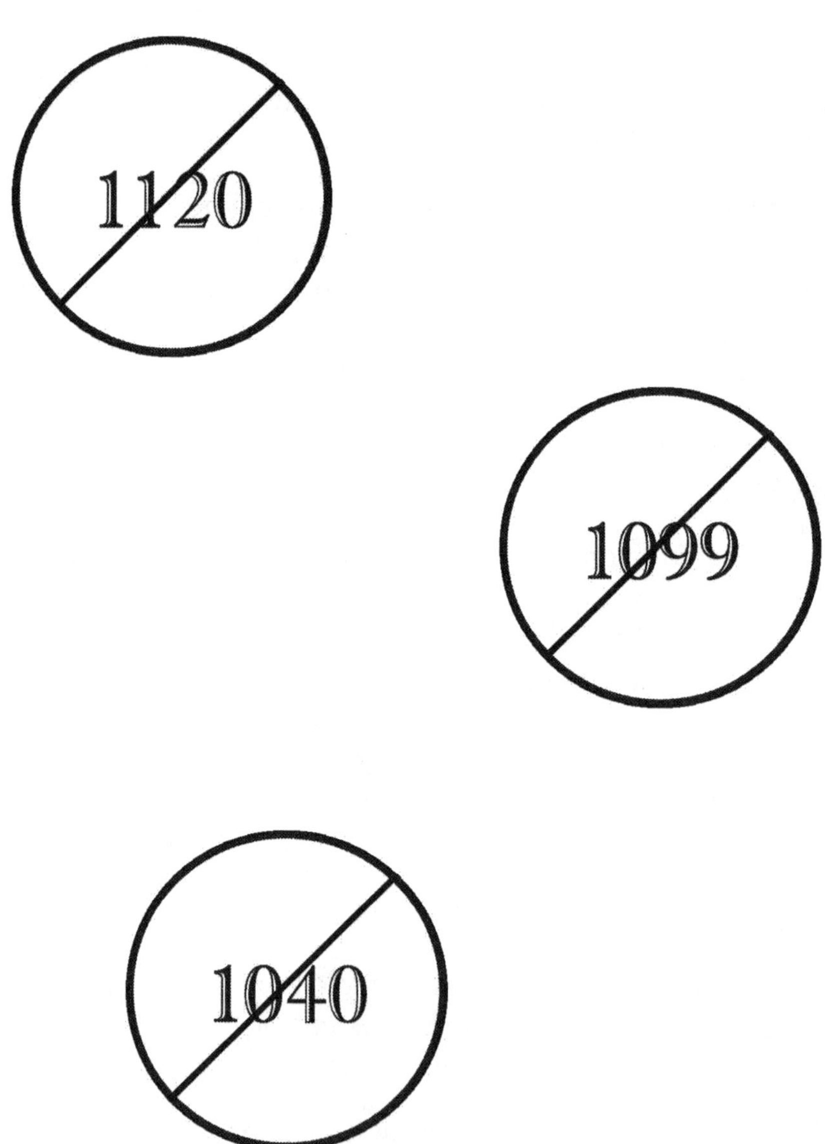

Chapter Three

The Demise of the IRS

If the idea of a transaction tax was followed faithfully it would basically eliminate the ponderous bureaucracy known as the IRS. The mistakes made by this government-formed monster are legion. They crucify some taxpayers and let others get away with a virtual slap on the wrist for virtually the same offense. I have seen varying estimates of the amount of uncollected income taxes that are on the government books today and it is mind-boggling. Then when you add the estimated taxes evaded it adds up to a figure that is outright ridiculous. Tax avoidance is legal but there are so many conflicting regulations nowadays that no possible transformation or reorganization of the IRS could possibly cure the problem of legal tax evasion.

Several years ago I attended an IRS-sponsored seminar projecting the bureau's plans for the future into the twenty-first century. They had purchased some forty million dollars worth of computers and planned to put one on the desk of every auditor (and every collector, evidently.) It all sounded so good! We left the seminar with the idea that perhaps the IRS was finally going to be able to enforce the tax laws in a manner that would justify their existence. Later, the whole idea died. Not enough of their auditors could operate computers, the data base required to put all tax returns (for ten years) at the fingertips of all agents was so vast, that it was very impractical.

Another interesting thing happened at this seminar. A regional Director of Internal Revenue gave t a talk about penalties and interest assessed and collected by the IRS. His statement was that his bosses in Washington, D.C. seemed to be more interested in collecting interest and penalties than they were in collecting income taxes. The reason was that interest and penalties were non-refundable in case a tax decision was overturned later. I have never heard of that Director again. He was transferred shortly after that to some other district (or Siberia).

Some of the bad effects of the incidents just mentioned, however, have been mitigated by the so-called Taxpayer's Bill of Rights that has been in effect for some years now. The IRS is desperately trying to look accountable for the first time in its existence. They know that the graduated income tax system is nearly inoperable in today's world.

Bureaucrats will detest the idea of a simpler form of taxation, you can be sure. They will decry the terrible loss of jobs (hundreds of thousands, probably), they will try to keep as many of their employees as possible, possibly to collect the billions of dollars of back taxes owed. Good try. And, they will succeed, to a point. Many billions of the back tax liabilities can be collected over the first ten years of the transaction tax, and then the IRS collection agency can be reduced to a very minor status in the taxing process. We, the people, will be our own tax collectors.

Chapter Four

Tax Collection Inadequacies

I doubt that anyone knows within many hundreds of millions of dollars how much money is owed the government in back income taxes. It is such a large sum the average person can hardly believe it. I have seen estimates running into the hundreds of millions and even hundreds of billions of dollars. This is what is owed according to filed returns or other determinations. This doesn't include the great unknown figure of taxable income not reported in the first place. This figure must be even more mind-boggling.

It sounds like such a small thing when the siding contractor or the roofing contractor, or the lawn service asks for cash because they need it for some particular purpose. No one thinks much of this and they pay cash with no withholding deducted for income tax. Much of the time these cash payments never find their way into the official receipts shown on the tax return of the business at year's end and the tax system just lost a few more dollars. This practice was supposedly stopped or at least stymied when the IRS started the 1099 reporting system. It wasn't, and only got worse. Individuals are not required to report on 1099s and a healthy discount will encourage the homeowner or other individual to hire the contractor or handyman in a flash. This practice is not restricted to homeowners, actually. It is a very pervasive practice in almost all or our society today, especially in service businesses.

Then there is the problem of the outright tax dodger who just doesn't file returns at all. Occasionally the IRS sets up an example of someone who is especially bad but literally thousands of people get a slap on the wrist if they ever get caught, pay some negligence penalty amount and go right back to their old ways. I know of several cases that occurred in just this way and to my knowledge the culprits are still not paying taxes.

The collection division of the IRS really has a terribly difficult assignment. Millions and millions of dollars are just right there for the collecting but in such small amounts in many cases that the cost of collection is more than the balance due. The computer has eased this problem considerably by a formal demand letter composed, written and mailed by the computer and sent by registered mail is frightening enough to most people that they will hastily send in the amount demanded, sometimes knowing that it is not correct. Most people doe not want the IRS looking over their shoulder so will pay tax and penalties up to a few hundred dollars rather than face a real, live IRS auditor or collector. After all, it might be quicker and simpler (and less expensive) to just pay the erroneous bill that to make waves by hiring a tax lawyer or CPA to fight the case. You might lose and have to pay your hired experts <u>and</u> the IRS.

Many of the amounts owed the government are forgiven merely because the IRS doesn't have be staff or resources required to collect the back taxes. An article in the Washington Post March 2004 revealed that the government had forgiven more than 2.2 million tax accounts totaling some 16.5 billion dollars. This was blamed on having a short staff and a restricted operating budget.

Compare all these problems with a transaction tax, low percentage, collected by businesses just like a sales tax is collected in the states having a sales tax.

No returns to file, no deductions, no exemptions, easy to understand, fair to all and no invasion of privacy.

One of the biggest problems found in the graduated income tax system is the social control built into the system. The political advocates of a social control factor built into the taxing system would still have some social control in the sense that they would possibly be able to control expenditures but not the tax collection process.

I have often wondered why ACLU activist lawyers haven't attacked the IRS on the grounds of invasion of privacy and economic discrimination. I have seen many of their attacks on frivolous matters far less important to my way of thinking.

Chapter Five

Accounting and Auditing IRS Style

There was a time before the income tax began to control the economy that the certified public accountant title stood for integrity and trust. Audits were dependable instruments in extending credit and making investment decisions. Bankers made loans based on financial statements that reflected factual information vouched for by the accountants issuing the reports.

The time came, however, that the authors of the Internal Revenue Code, namely our Congress, began to re-write all the old established accounting rules and took away all the ability of the accounting profession to use tried and true methods of measuring the value of a business or professional enterprise.

The first major problem the income tax encountered in the early days was the problem of depreciation and depletion. So, why the problem? Depreciation had always been a problem for auditors even before income tax but solidifying it into a taxing tool was a real problem. This resulted in thousands of tax audits and lawsuits over many years. It also resulted in creating a feeling in the financial community that accounting statements that didn't match up with tax returns were possibly not good for lending purposes. How could a banker look at a farm's balance sheet and see a minimal balance left in depreciable equipment and yet have the farmer tell him that he had equipment actually worth thousands of dollars more than that? Who is the banker to believe?

In different sections of the country another problem arose but was stopped early on due to some brainy hero of the resource extraction industry (you spell that as OIL). This originally started, as I recall, in Texas. The oil barons of the day were making big bucks early in the war years and their tax bills were distressing to say the least. So, they finally came up with the deduction of "depletion". I haven't heard any arguments about depletion in many years now but what it amounts to, simply, is a deduction out of thin air that supposedly reimburses the taxpayer for the depletion of his wasting asset, an oil lease, for example. Since the taxpayer is also deducting all development costs and lease payments it almost looks like a real live tax dodge, doesn't it?

So many tax credits and other "sweetheart" deductions have gone through the tax code that has, in many instances, cancelled each other. Pressure groups and special interest group lobbies have inserted little innocuous-sounding sentences into major legislation and have seen their groups prosper from the tax savings involved.

One of the major concerns since the first days of the income tax was the double taxation involved when a corporation distributed its profits to shareholders in the form of dividends. Remember, the corporation has already paid tax once on its profits so why should the shareholder pay again? The problem was finally fixed to a degree, at least, by creation of a legal creature called a Sub-chapter S corporation. This was a purely tax-generated entity that was neither fish nor fowl. It allowed a qualified corporation to be treated for tax purposes as though it were a partnership so that operating profits and losses would be passed through to the shareholders without the double taxation of a 'C' corporation.

The trouble with the 'S' corporation in the early days was that, generally speaking, taxpayers didn't take it seriously. They were intrigued by the supposed lack of personal liability they had had in their un-incorporated business before and the ability to deduct corporate losses on their personal returns. What could be better? However, the 'S' corporation rules didn't seem to impress them enough to exercise discipline rules such as director's meetings, annual meetings, and careful attention to keeping minutes and such. This resulted in a lot of additional revenue for the IRS in penalties and interest.

Many of the shareholders of small 'S' corporations had a very blurred vision as far as personal use of company vehicles, titling of property of all kinds, etc. "After all, it's my car," the owner would say, "I own the corporation. I can drive it across the U.S. on my vacation if I want to." So, there!

Incidents such as this and many more got the graduated income tax system to the stage it is in today, a mess. Unbelievable, stupendous amounts of tax money go unpaid because of confusing and misunderstood rules and regulations. Most taxpayers won't or don't want to spend the many dollars that an accountant or other tax consultant must charge in order to keep up with all the conflicting rules and regulations.

Chapter Six

Look at all that money!

Over the past decade we have been awash with money in this country. The monetary policy in the 90's was so liberal that money was coming out our ears, in a manner of speaking. The budget was finally balanced (supposedly) by the old method politicians usually balance the budgets, print cheap dollars to pay the bills. This is an over-simplification of a much more complex problem but it boils down to the same basic solution.

How our dollars get spread around the world is amazing. Bales and trunks of U.S. currency totaling in the hundreds of millions were found by U.S. troops in Iraq. How did it get there? Was it subjected to income tax the way U.S. citizen/taxpayers are? It had to represent income to someone, didn't it?

You know and I know that drug pushers don't pay Income tax. The income tax advocates of the 1930's have made a big thing of catching Al Capone by use of the income tax and they played on that feat for many years. It created good PR for the income tax (they desperately needed it) but it did nothing to made the tax fair or equitable even from the beginning.

But, let's get back to the talk of money. How do you calculate the amount of tax to expect if you tax transactions instead of net income? For that matter, calculating the expected amount of "net taxable" income must be a problem, itself. One could use bank deposits, less non-countable deposits such as government deposits and personal transfer deposits and calculate that the tax would have been 1% of the net figure. Our final estimated figure was approximately 3.5-4.0 trillion dollars, which would be sufficient to fuel the nation's economy nicely, thank you.

Actually, this would be the work of Congressional economists, accountants and statisticians. They have an immensely more elaborate data base to work with and they would probably end up with a new, closely targeted tax factor each year. I have kept my figures to an even percentage factor for simplification purposes. But the money is there, all in that huge tax base that grows yearly as population grows. Another note of interest is that a transaction tax automatically adjusts for inflation. This has always been a factor with the income tax.

As an example of the tremendous amount of money floating in our economy a newspaper article in the Twin Falls, Idaho *Times-News* November 7, 2004, showed that bank deposits of four smaller independent banks in that southern Idaho area had total deposits in the third quarter of 2004 in a total amount of over $887. million dollars. This, I stress, did not include any of the larger chain banks' deposits.

Of course, the largest single area for collecting the transaction tax would be the securities and commodities markets. Now, before I get a cry of outrage from stockbrokers and investors let me say this. If you can stay away from all the record-keeping the income tax requires and you escape the sometimes horrendous tax effects of your profits, aren't you far and away ahead of the game?

The securities and commodities markets are volatile and unpredictable as to profits for the participants but would on balance provide a steady flow of tax funds and would not harm the general economy. These markets would also create the windfall tax income discussed in another chapter of this book. There might be some outcry from foreign interests but they would almost be forced to invest in our markets because with the UTT tax in force our dollar would almost certainly increase in value. We would regain the dominant position we have almost lost with the economic strain the graduated income tax has put on our economy.

The following chart reflects a tiny percentage of one day's results of our major stock markets. It shows the results of the fifteen most active stocks on our three major market divisions and shows the amount of UTT tax that would have resulted from these few stocks. There are thousands of stocks available in dozens of different locations in the United States plus commodity exchanges so it is easy to imagine the daily tax income the U.S. Treasury would receive with the UTT tax in force.

Total Dollar Value of 15 most active stocks listed on NYSE, AMEX and Nasdaq, November 24, 2004

Stock	Volume	Closing Price	Dollar Value	1% UTT Tax
Lucent	343749	4.00	1374996.00	13749.96
Pfizer	317107	26.61	8438217.27	84382.1727
TimeWarner	286353	17.94	5137172.82	51371.7282
NortelNif	257501	3.17	816278.17	8162.7817
Motorola	210638	18.87	3974739.06	39747.3906
Nasd100Tr	895834	39.00	34937526.00	349375.26
SPDR	403668	118.2	47713557.60	477135.576
SemiHTr	155185	33.27	5163004.95	51630.0495
IShR2000	108118	124.87	13500694.66	135006.9466
DJIADian	14412	104.98	1512971.76	15129.7176
Sinuss	4169197	6.71	27975311.87	279753.1187
Intel	910778	23.37	21284881.86	212848.8186
Microsoft	814163	26.53	21599744.39	215997.4439

Cisco	441006	19.0	8379114.00	83791.14
ApldMall	306263	16.9	5175844.70	51758.447
Totals			206984055.10	2069840.551

The listing above whose a typical day's collections of the UTT tax from a tiny section of the stock and securities market. Thousands of stocks are active each day along with bonds and other securities and commodities.

I must point out again that the UTT tax makes no distinction between winners and losers. He who pays the money pays the tax so the "buyer" has already paid his tax. It's a done deal and the taxpayers are not participating in his loss in the manner they are with the graduated income tax.

As I said in a previous chapter it will take a much larger data base and a larger complement of personnel than I can muster to compute the actual final percentage rate of the UTT tax. From the research I have done and from what others have stated the one percent figure will provide more than enough funds to cover whatever reasonable budget the country comes up with.

Even if our preliminary figures are all wrong there is no possible way that the rate would be more than three percent. And, in light of the seventeen percent called for in a national sales tax proposal or the twenty-one or twenty-three percent for a flat tax proposal even three percent looks like a bargain.

Chapter Seven

Home, Sweet Home!

In the late 90's some taxpayers who had good tax consultants found a way to make a lot of tax-free money. It was one of the best tax breaks to come along in decades and was a preface to the Bush tax cut program. This was a bonanza waiting to happen. The tax break not only made money for a lot of people, it has led to a spurring of the economy that was hailed by almost all politicians, liberal and conservative. It helped greatly to relieve the so-called recession during President Bush's first term. Actually, the Bush tax cuts were "revenue neutral" but the tax relief that was most effective was the one giving taxpayers the right to sell their principal residence tax-free if they had actually lived in the house for at least two years. Lots of fine print, also, but that was (and is) the basic law.

With the population increase we have had in the United States over the past twenty or thirty years the price of existing homes had risen steadily since the 50's and 60's. Urban sprawl had sent bare land prices higher by the year, Zoning ordinances and Environmental Protection Agency rules also forced prices higher in many cases. The new tax change came at just the right time. The residence that many retiring taxpayers had bought near L.A. or San Jose or Denver or Boston back in 1962 or thereabouts for maybe $60,000.00 was now worth $450,000.00. The problem over the years was that people would have had to pay not only commissions and other selling costs upon a sale of the residence but also hefty Federal and sometimes state income taxes on the profit. Suddenly, they can sell and have no tax at all upon sales, only sales commissions.

So, they sold out and moved to a lesser market area, say the lake country in the Ozarks or somewhere they liked to retire. They bought a home, probably as large as the one they had sold. They paid perhaps $125,000.00 for this new home but they only put $15,000.00 down and financed the balance over, say, 30 years and a reasonable rate of interest. They then have $435,000.00 <u>in cash</u> to retire with. With their social security and possibly 401(k) distributions life is great. Now, the kicker. After they have lived in this retirement home for two years they find that they can get $200,000.00 for it. So, perhaps they sell again and pick up another profit of ^$50-60,000.00. They can do this every two years until they have accumulated $250,000.00 each in their lifetimes. (Ed. note: This changed in 2004. Now there is no limit on accumulation of profits on sale of home in a lifetime.)

All of these bonanza tax laws are patched into a flawed system that is completely out of date and is so cumbersome that it is almost impossible for the Congress to make appropriations that will do the jobs that need to be done and stay within whatever budget that can be predicted.

Don't get me wrong. Some of the tax breaks have been for very good causes and have caused may people to do good things for their communities that they would never have done just out of the goodness of their hearts. The fairly generous credits for restoring and preserving our older historic buildings have been a credit to our country. So, some good has come from the complex patchwork of conflicting laws to somewhat counteract the bad.

By and large, home ownership is one thing that everyone, almost without exception, trumpets as a paragon of good economics for all families. The buildup of equity in a home will, by monthly payment after monthly payment, a form of savings; one of the best there is, in fact. Home ownership is one thing that is typically American and one of the things that does not exist in large measure in much of the rest of the world.

All of these platitudes are well and good but don't get into trouble with the IRS. Your happy home life can be shattered if an IRS collector gets you in his sights and decides to make you life miserable. He usually cannot kick you out of your house but he can make your life miserable. Your home is not your castle ever again until you "pay the piper". All kinds of publicity can result in your circle of neighbors and friends. In one case the offending taxpayer was "shadowed" by the collector even when he drove his children to school, went to the grocery store and would get in line at the grocery store to see how he paid for the groceries. The IRS finally won and the taxpayer lost his home. Actually, in this case, the taxpayer was guilty of not paying the payroll taxes assessed against his small business. So, this was somewhat different than non-payment of income tax, this was a greater no-no, that of withholding "trust funds" from the government. The taxpayer Bill of Rights did not help the taxpayer.

I hardly think that a deduction for home mortgage interest should be the reason for keeping a decrepit and bumbling system but that is always one of the biggest objections to changing the system. Actually, in the case of most middle-class taxpayers the deduction for home loan interest would only save them $500.00 to $700.00 in actual tax. What would the homeowner's tax be under the UTT tax? On a home of $150,000.00 the tax would be $1,500.00 (once, at closing upon purchase) and <u>nothing</u> after that.

Is this going to cause problems by making home ownership less desirable? I doubt it. I think it would cause some competition among lenders and cause interest rates to be more competitive but I don't believe that it would discourage the "own you own home" ethic that is imbedded in the American psyche.

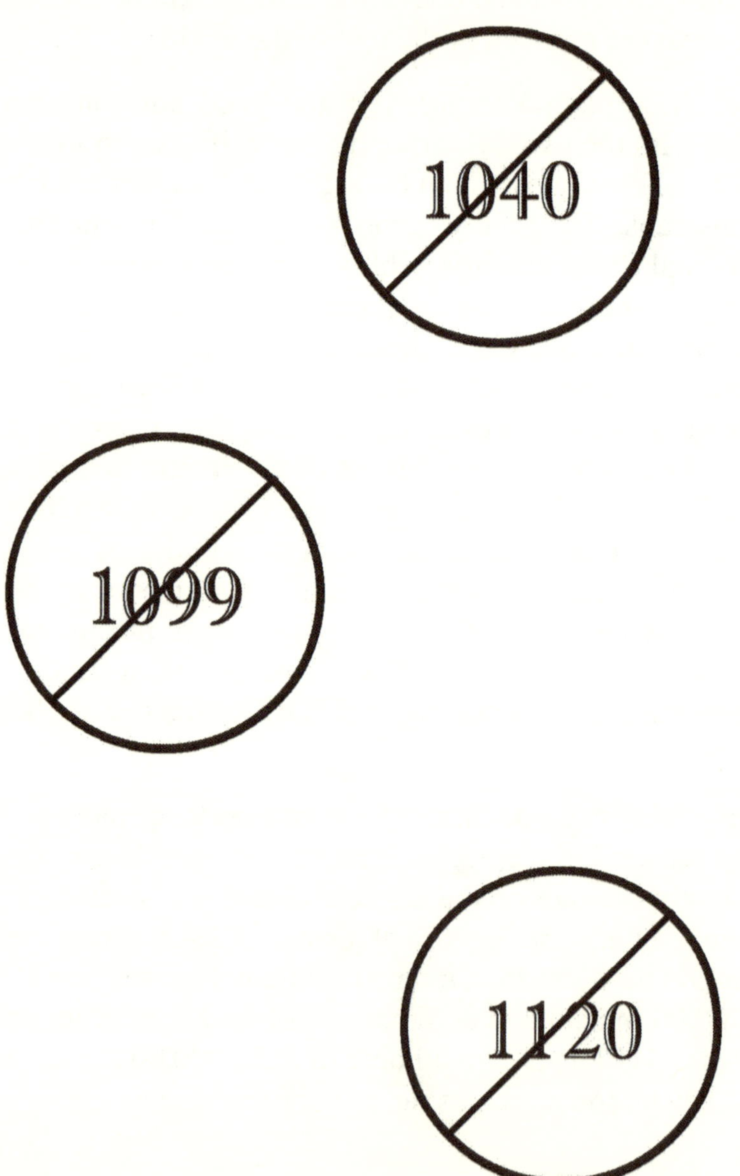

Chapter Eight

Which Shell is the Pea Under?

The old shell game is still operating for some of our politicians. Now, many of them use different figures to prove a point during their speeches but some is like the old time hucksters' singsong chants.

There reason for this is that the government has different methods of accounting in use for different purposes. They quote different figures for different reasons. There is a set of figures for budgetary purposes and another for annual reporting figures. One is on the accrual basis and another is on the dash basis. The budgetary year is on a fiscal year basis and taxes are estimated on a calendar year basis (I think). Actually, I doubt if either of these figures are correct under strict accounting rules.

The budgetary figures are fiscal year estimates and these figures are the ones the politicians argue over so fitfully when the usual deficit amount is announced there is always the eternal argument about tax budget cuts and pork barrel expenditures and all the time they are talking about tremendous amount of money that is being estimated. Later in the year, figures come out that are announced (presumably on the cash basis) that alter the original estimates up or down. These are greeted with glee by the prevailing administration and usually ignored by the opposition party.

I have never been able to settle on a sense of timing with all these enormous figures. If the budget is on a fiscal year and our income taxes are on a mostly calendar year (except for type C corporations, of course), where does my tax payment on April 15, 2005 apply? If I had a windfall profit in 2004 and pay the tax in 2006 by use of extensions, etc., does he Treasury keep amending their figures for the 2004 budget? How can estimates even begin to be believable that are ten years in the future when we can't even "get it right" for one year in advance?

In the mid-90's Congress was putting enormous pressure on President Clinton to "balance the budget". For several years they hounded him unmercifully. He and his advisors repeatedly said it couldn't be done before 2000 or later. Finally, through a number of financial maneuvers it did happen over a rather short period of time. President Clinton was hailed as the financial genus of the decade by his supporters and life went on. But it has always seemed to me to be only a matter of confidence in the taxpayers' minds whether the budget was actually balanced or not. I, like most taxpayers, were too busy trying to pay our ever-increasing tax bills to worry about it very much. Did his budgets actually balance? I don't know whether they did or not. It seems to me that over the near-decade of his administration the national debt increased a lot more than the deficits he showed less the announced surpluses.

While talking of shell games we must visit the most famous of all, the Social Security Trust Fund. This is the supposed "lock-box" full of money that has been paid in by workers over many years and "invested" for their retirements. Wrong. This is a file cabinet, or a battery of them, that is full of government bonds. A safe investment? Certainly, the best in the world. But part of the "national debt? You bet! So, here we have a real paradox, an item that is both an asset and a liability. But, as one ardent supporter told mce once, "What's the difference? It's our money" Go figure!

A change of taxing methods from the graduated income tax to the UTT tax would broaden the tax base to the ultimate limit and yet keep the tax rate at very acceptable levels. The present levels of payroll tax could be kept in force for a few years in order to build the reserves that reportedly are needed in 2018. The only thing that is needed to "fix" social security is money, I think, and the UTT tax would cover that problem admirable. Some concessions could even be made to build larger reserves for those lower-income workers.

A similar situation exists in the Highway Trust Fund, I believe. I would assume that that file cabinet is also stuffed with the asset/liabilities securities. Which shell is the pea under?

Actually, my former statement is true, that the government securities are the safest investment around. But, on the other hand, it brings up the memory that way down deep all politicians like a moderate bit of inflation over the years. Inflation creates cheap dollars to pay off governments someday far down the road of time and long after the politician is gone.

The UTT tax is immediate and simple. It is easy to understand and logical in its application. And there is no question as to which shell the pea is under. It's under all the shells.

Chapter Nine

It's a State of Mind

One of the biggest problems I foresee involving the acceptance of the UTT tax is that of the different states of the Union. Almost all of the different states have a mélange of income tax and/or a sales tax. Many of the states have both. The states with both have huge collection problems and the burden of bureaucratic cost of collection of both taxes surely must devour a huge part of the final collection amount.

I'm sure that some of the states would at first oppose the idea of the federal government collecting their tax but the UTT tax could be very easily refund part of their total collection back to the states and relieve the states of many of their collection woes.

The taxpayers of the states might be somewhat perturbed if they kept their state income tax rate of six to eight percent or so and see their federal government only taxing at a 1% rate or paying a sales tax of six to ten percent while the federal government was charging one percent or so for the UTT tax. I doubt that state elected officials could withstand the voter pressure that would result from opposition to the UTT tax replacing such high rates as exist in the states.

Some of the state administrations might oppose the UTT tax system as an imposition on states' rights but this is not a valid argument in my view. There are already many instances of Federal/state joint collections, such as the FUTA tax collections mentioned earlier. The tax could be divided by the software at the bank collection software. This doesn't sound like the best idea, however.

Under the UTT tax system, probably four or five states would collect the most tax. New York State would probably lead the pack in tax collected because of all the securities sales and population spending. Illinois, California, Texas, Florida would also handle a larger percentage of total funds. Congress would have to formulate an equitable system of distribution of the overall tax so that mid-western and other small states received enough to cover their budgets after the abandonment of their income and sales tax programs. Federal mandates to the states could then be channeled to the states through the UTT distribution system.

The different states have brought many of their problems upon themselves. In some cases poor planning has resulted in financial problems. In other cases social control measures have created enormous problems. Some states blame their problems on their having to fulfill Federal mandates with either delayed funding or lack of funding by the Federal government.

The states have also built mountainous problems by installing unbelievable bureaucratic regimes. Some state income and sales tax regulations are so riddled with pressure group exemptions and deductions that it is a wonder that the state treasury is still solvent. And, strangely enough, it is much easier for a state tax collector to go on a fishing expedition through a business bank account than it is for an IRS agent to do the same thing. I have found over the years that dealing with state auditors and tax collectors is much harder than dealing with the IRS auditors. You might notice that I haven't added IRS collection agents to that list. They can be quite ornery at times. Not as bad as some years ago, though, before the Taxpayers' Bill of Rights.

One of the main problems with states' taxing systems is that each state has a different attorney general and these people are a bunch of individualists. Most of the social control features built into state tax law is put there by some attorney general at some point in time. Once this little blurb is installed in the system it, like any bureaucratic measure, stays there forever. It gets imbedded and no one ever has the political or moral courage to remove it. In a state with heavy agricultural interests farmers, for example, do not have to pay sales tax on farm supplies. Those are considered costs of production and exempt. And there, again, it is a matter of definition. It is like the old adage, "There are two kinds of people in the world, the sane and the insane, and the sane ones do the classifying." Go figure.

Probably the best method of rebating UTT tax funds to the states would be by population. This, on the surface, seems fair and equitable but it must be left to Congress to figure this out. The UTT tax could certainly provide enough funds to do everything needed and still relieve the states of massive personnel costs and the costs of both their personal costs but also business costs such as vehicles, travel, etc

Many of the states having an income tax have modeled enabling statutes on the Federal Tax Code, some of them using the adjusted gross income per the Federal return and computing the state tax from there. This is all fine and good for a the first few years then the state legislators, needing more revenue, started tinkering with little gimmicks and soon the simple little state income tax return is almost as hard to prepare as the Federal rerun. We have inadvertently created some thirty or forty separate income tax codes. This is a nightmare for many taxpayers in the northeast. Many of them live in one state and work in another. Maybe their wives work in even another state.

What a nightmare. I would imagine there are a lot of people who would endorse the idea of a UTT tax!

And talk about diversity! Try preparing a return for a construction worker, perhaps, who works in, say, four or five different states during a year. Some of the states have an income tax, others don't. When the taxpayer sees his bill from the preparer he won't believe it took so much time. The most horrendous example of this I have ever encountered was when a taxpayer worked in three states, Idaho, Vermont and Massachusetts. What a struggle! Vermont has no income tax, Idaho's tax is somewhat based on the Federal tax return but Massachusetts must have a tax code committee that does most of their work in a daze. It was a terrible job even though most of it was done on computer.

One tax not imposed by the Federal government is the use tax. This tax is only, to my knowledge, used by the states that have sales taxes, to catch those horrible people who go out of state to buy something in another state that has less (or no) sales tax charged. Of late, the focus has been on people who deal with internet sales or purchases. Millions of dollars have been spent in an all-out effort to get sales or use taxes paid but there is no easy way to collect these taxes. But, look, folks, the UTT tax program take care of this automatically. Everyone had to put money (or credit cards) into the bank, don't they? Go figure!

Some states, in a frenzy of despair over shrinking tax revenues and expanding budgets have contracted with tax SWAT teams to collect sales and use taxes. If one of these teams comes into your business don't expect to sleep well for quite awhile. If they come to audit a particular year and find that you have misinterpreted the law they can go back for up to ten years and forward to the current year an assume that you have always been at fault. The bill will be utterly stupendous. Ask any accountant that has been through one of these all-out audits and he will tell you that sales and use tax audits are infinitely worse than Federal income tax audits. And the state tax departments, especially the sales and use tax divisions, don't seem to have any "dead" years. Federal income tax returns have an expiration date of three years from the date the return was due. I haven't found this to be true with state governments.

The UTT tax would take the heat off state tax authorities and would also drastically cut the state's costs of collection. Also, like the Federal monies, the funds would be there immediately rather than 18-24 months later. And the states would share in the broader tax base enjoyed by the Federal government. It would appear to be a win-win situation.

Chapter Ten

Trading and Bartering

A significant portion of the real estate market today is comprised of real estate trades. These trades are under the auspices of the Tax Code Section 1031. They can be amazingly simple and are tax-free if done correctly. You must deal through an independent facilitator who handles all the paperwork and any money that is involved. The real estate agents are paid by the facilitator and all the title work, registrations, etc. are handled by him, also. The routine has been streamlined over the years and is a beautiful way to dispose of low-basis properties without suffering a sometimes brutal tax trap.

You can "trade down" at present, trading, for example, a $400,000.00 apartment house for a $200,000.00 four-plex and taking $200,000.00 (less expenses, loans, etc.) to the bank. It isn't quite that simple, however. You will face the usual number of red-tape difficulties but they can be overcome and you have "traded down" into a smaller property and you haven't faced the awful tax you would have paid on an outright sale of the larger property.

There are many, many of these trades going on these days and the Section 1031 trade is tremendously popular. However, there is one little glitch that people don't think about at first. There is the restriction that you must trade "like for like" in properties. For example, you can't trade appreciated securities for an apartment house.

Realtors I have talked to have asked how the UTT tax would affect these trades. I have had to tell them that it would obviate the tax effect which has been their trademark for many years. On the other hand, the UTT tax would take away the restriction of "like for like" that currently hurts many trades. I feel that there would be many more trades made just as economic trades rather than as a tax maneuver. Three- and four-way trades would flourish, I believe. I know that I have had innumerable inquiries over the years from clients desiring to trade houses for motorhomes, or the reverse, or even a herd of horses for a silver mine.

Trades made after initiation of the UTT tax would have to have dollar values assigned for tax purposes by the facilitator and collection of the tax would be made by him at the time of closing. Actually, in a trade, all participating trade entities are both buyers and sellers, so, in keeping with the reasoning behind the UTT tax the "seller" pays the tax. Simple, no complications and economic activity is spurred by removal of a plethora of regulations and rules.

There is another area in the trading field that deserves some attention and that lies in the area of trading stamps, discount coupons and barter companies.

Trading stamps are almost a thing of the past, having been almost taxed out of existence by escheat laws of the various states. So, I will treat them much as I treat the discount coupon industry. These should all be handled in the same way that they are usually handled by the states that have sales tax on foodstuffs. The tax is charged on the total purchase amount before the coupon amount is deducted. The UTT tax would be so tiny in most cases that this would not affect the tax appreciably, in any case.

Another question I need to address is that of merchandise giveaways and that biggie, the LOTTERY! Could the government ever resist taking a large chunk out of lottery winnings and drop back to a paltry one- or two-percent? On this one, I have no call. This would require Congressional decision. As far as merchandise giveaways, the UTT tax might be considered part of the advertising or PR cost and paid by the sponsor. Again, I would await approval by Congress.

I have been a proponent of trade transactions for many years. In my personal dealings in real estate and especially personal property I have never failed to think about possible trades. Sometimes, that little addition to a sale advertisement has led to an avenue not explored by others and has led me to a result that I wouldn't have expected otherwise.

The UTT tax would certainly not hurt the trading picture and elimination of the income tax just might spur the trading idea into a significant increase of sales.

Chapter Eleven

Price Structuring and the UTT Tax

The Universal Transaction Tax incorporates features of both the Value Added (VAT) and the typical sales tax. Both theses tax strategies have been pushed by different Congressional reformers of the out-dated and generally condemned graduated income tax. Both have also been castigated by most American tax students as impractical and, without a general increase in the tax base, far too expensive to sell to the voters/taxpayers.

The VAT adds to the retail price incrementally. For example, as I understand it, a manufacturer of widgets would pay out, say, $300.00 to complete a product. He would pay, perhaps, a 10% VAT tax when he bought the materials and labor for the completed product so he now has $330.00 invested. He then sells the product to a wholesaler for $770.00 which includes another $70.00 VAT tax. The wholesaler then sells the product to a retailer for $1,100.00 which includes $100.00 VAT tax. The retailer then sells the product to a buyer for $1,500.00 which includes, roughly, another $135.00 VAT tax. So, the taxing authority gets a whopping $365.00 tax on $1,500.00 in sales, amounting to a 24% tax rate, it seems to me. As you can see, unless the tax base is significantly broadened it is almost impossible to impose a VAT on an educated group of taxpayers.

The VAT tax is imposed all the way up the sales ladder with the tax added in at each level. This balloon effect adds to prices but is more-or-less hidden from the ultimate consumer of products. It would have fewer incremental points as far as services are concerned. Not having dealt with the VAT tax directly, I cannot profess to be any authority on any of the intricate rules in the system but I have been told by people who have dealt with it that the paperwork trail is a horrendous chore for business to cope with. The tax is only imposed on business and professionals, as I understand it, so, evidently the ultimate taxpayer shrugs and pays it. I don't know if any of the European countries using the VAT system also have an income tax.

I was in London on a company-sponsored tour in the mid-90's when I first encountered the VAT. Our rooms and transportation were paid by the company but we paid for our own food, beverages and personal purchases. I was advised to keep track of all these items by keeping receipts and that I could apply for refund of all the VAT paid, since I was not a British taxpayer. I sent all the supposedly required forms back to London after arriving home but never heard anything from the VAT at all. I think the figure was about $95.00. I wonder where that money went.

State sales taxes in the United States are so messy and vary so much in their sometimes senseless deductions and exemptions that I certainly would not recommend a Federal sales tax system. What a clash of paperwork we would have if we superimposed a 23% Federal sales tax onto an already-staggering 6-10% state sales tax! Different exemptions and deductions, different sales requirements such as out-of-state sales. What a horrible mess that would be for small businesses and also the governments themselves.

When considering price structures and tax system change, we are obligated to protect the economy as well as produce tax revenues. Of late we have been exposed too much publicity about changing the tax system to a national sales tax. The rates of tax mentioned are from 17-23%. Now, let's use a bit of reality. The automobile business is of paramount importance in the country and auto sales are vital to our economy whether we approve or not. Let' say that we adopt a national sales tax of 23%. You go downtown to the auto dealer to buy a new car. So the salesperson says, "Yep, got this little honey right here. Just what you want, it will only cost you $20,000.00 today. Well, actually, there is sales tax on it. That will be $4,600.00 for Federal tax and another $1,200.00 for state tax. Lovely car you bought!"

The conversation might cool your ardor for buying a new car. How many conversations of this sort would it take before the economy went flat? For that reason alone we must take great care in changing our outmoded tax system.

It is hard to say whether the UTT system would lower prices. The market place would undoubtedly automatically adjust somewhat to a lower built-in tax rate but lessening the profit restraint on business by ridding ourselves of the graduated income tax might not lower prices, only keep profits at a bit higher level. Conversely, if the graduated income tax were gone, perhaps many business managers would slash prices in order to achieve a larger customer base and more dollar volume.

Examples of Tax Income Potential:

1) A standard washing machine, produced in the U.S.A.:

Manufacturer buys parts, materials to Build washer, estimated at $300.	Tax paid	$3.00
Distributor buys washer from manufacturer, estimated $400.	Tax paid	$4.00

Dealer buys washer from Distributor, estimated $480.	Tax paid	$4.80
Customer buys washer from dealer, estimated $680.	Tax paid	$6.80
Total Transactions Taxed est. $1,860.	Total Tax	$18.60

2) An automobile:

Distributor buys auto from manufacturer, estimated $9,000,	Tax Paid	$90.00
Dealer buys auto from distributor, estimated $11,000.	Tax Paid	$110.00
Customer buys auto from dealer, estimated $15,000.	Tax Paid	$150.00
Total Transactions $35,000.	Total Tax	$350.00

Note: Above figures are for illustration of the VAT type figures only. They have no basis in fact as to prices or margins of profit in industry.

Chapter Twelve

Payroll Taxes and a Monumental Puzzle, Social Security

Mention payroll taxes to a group of people and there is an immediate outcry about the severity of their impact on the average workers' paychecks. Few people automatically connect payroll taxes with Social Security and Medicare benefits. A couple of my grandsons brought their W-2 forms from their first jobs in to me and were aghast when I told them that not all of their withheld taxes would be refunded to them. They couldn't understand why they, at age 16 or so, had to pay into a supposed fund that would pay them something some forty or fifty years later. I had a hard time explaining it to them when I hadn't really answered all my questions over many years.

My first problem with Social Security tax being withheld from my paychecks came many years ago when I first encountered the tax and found that it was not a voluntary savings device. Even them I knew that the fund was not a "lock-box" fund and that benefits were being paid even then to recipients who had paid very little into the fund.

The Social Security program has never been and never will be, actuarially sound. Many people, even today, try to profile the plan as a retirement system, when, even by the original founders in the 1930's, it was not designed that way. It is a supplemental program only.

There were, and are still, so many unanswered questions about Social Security that few people under age 50 feel that they will get any benefits at all from the program. What an actuarial nightmare it must be to try to estimate future benefits, requirements, etc! For example, what of the tremendous costs of administering the program? Who pays them? A lifelong bachelor, beginning at age 20, will pay in the same amount of money as another worker who married at age 22 but the married worker will draw Social Security and his wife will also draw up to seventy-five percent of his check and she has paid in far less and maybe even no money at all.

Some years ago some bright tax tactician dreamed up a good way tfor the government to get some of "its" hard-earned Social Security money back from those middle-class retirees living it up in the sunshine. They imposed a tax on Social Security proceeds if all other income exceeded some $32,000.00 for a married couple. So, anyone who had worked and built any retirement income at all and perhaps worked part-time after retirement paid (usually) 15% of his Social Security checks back to the government. And, also, many of the taxpayers were quite a little above the 15% bracket so they were taxed at 28% or more.

In spite of all the complexities of the Social Security program it is still a tremendous protection for the elderly workers of our country. Little is said in favor of some of the other features of the program, such as the disability payment feature and the life insurance feature. These are highly desirable features and I have had many recipients of these funds tell me how wonderful they were in times of disability or unfortunate death.

"Fixing" Social Security should be easy. It only needs money. It could probably use some audit procedures, also, but that extends to most government programs, anyhow.

At this writing, though, the present administration is not concerned with the total "fix" for Social Security. They are pushing for another feature which would make the program much more sturdy and far-reaching. Also, their idea that of personal accounts for workers would build savings which any country needs in order to grow and sustain its populace.

Outright abolishment of payroll taxes immediately upon adoption of the UTT tax might be hard to sell to the taxpayer/ voters. It might have to wait until the UTT tax has shown to them that expansion of the tax base has done its job and that it could be done. Some compromise could be made whereby the government starts building the reserves in the so-called "Trust Fund" and present workers stay at their present level for a few years. Many, many arguments must yet be made.

I feel that "fixing" Social Security should wait until, preferably, the UTT tax has been approved and adopted. Action prior to that is like "getting the cart before the horse". As I said earlier, all the system needs is money and that the UTT tax can provide.

Not only do payroll taxes affect the employed worker but what about the self-employed small-business person? He has to pay, not only his social security and Medicare portions of the tax but also the employer's portion, a total of 15.8% of his profits from his small business. This can boost him into a rather high bracket if he lives in a state charging a 6% sales tax and an 8% state income tax.

I had an interesting case a few years ago. A gentleman came in who had recently retired and wanted to start a small business. His wife had also retired from a longtime job. Both had some retirement income from their past jobs, were drawing social security plus hey owned a rental property that added to their income. As I remember, their total income, before social security was about $50,000.00. The small business would supposedly throw off profits of about $15,000.00 a year. The gentleman was astonished when I told him he would be paying taxes on that profit amount at a rate of over 50%. He hadn't realized he had a partner when he started his planning. He, understandably, didn't go into the small business.

This has happened thousands of times in the past few years. Anyone desiring to engage in a self-employment enterprise after retirement is severely penalized. They will probably have a 401(k) or something similar, some investment income or rental, and their social security. Perhaps they are in the 15% bracket until the self-employment income is added in then they immediately have tax liability for their social security and they have to pay self-employment tax of 15.2%. All of this bumps them into the 28% tax bracket, making it very expensive to engage in a small-business venture after retirement. This is probably contributory to the golf courses being so crowded nowadays.

There are certainly no easy answers to the social security problem. The system probably only needs money for its ailments. And it doesn't need that for a few years but it should be put on a sound basis for the future before public confidence is shaken.

Chapter Thirteen

Taking Care of Business

I think it is fair to say that multi-national corporations are probably some of the worst transgressors we have where income taxes are concerned. They can afford the best tax lawyers and accountants (also lobbyists) and can hide money in the best tax havens known to mankind. They can essentially pay off foreign third-world governments for business favors and then take credit for supposed "taxes" against their U.S. taxes. Now, this is not common. Many of our most respected multi-nationals observe the letter of the law but there are some that work exactly as I mentioned above. Payoffs are common in the third-world countries (in all the countries, actually) and American taxpayers foot the bill for many of the pay-offs. This has been documented my times over in recent years, even as recently as the reported United Nations Oil for Food program payoffs.

There should be some way under the UTT tax program that profits brought home from foreign subsidiaries or operations would be taxed as any other transaction would be but perhaps we would be getting back into a definition problem that we want to avoid by the UTT tax to begin with.

My main concern, however, is with small business. Most economic writers are not concerned with business taxes, it seems to me. They talk in valid terms about taxing people, about taxing the rich, not taxing savings and many other facets of the taxation question However, they don't bring up the fact that big business handles most of the cash flow of the United States and yet most of the income Tax Code manipulation deals with small business and individual tax issues.

Some years ago it was a beautiful tax dodge for a profitable corporation to find another corporation with a huge tax loss carry-forward, conduct a reverse merger (merging the profitable corporation into the loss corporation as though the loss corporation had purchased it) then change the name of the revitalized entity back to a name or logo the same or similar to the first corporation. This went on for many years and cost the taxpaying public many billions of dollars. I haven't heard of much of this in the last few years but I suppose it still goes on in one form or the other even today.

I must say that a host of regulations have been issued attempting to stop this practice but believe me, where there is a regulation there is an escape route somewhere. Now, what a crazy thing! Basically, they are again turning a liability (a tax loss) into a saleable asset. And the taxpayer is footing the bill!

The small business has no room to maneuver under the present income tax laws. Big business can, in most cases, raise prices or buy profits in advance by leaning heavily on suppliers but the small business cannot do that. The small business has little bargaining power on purchases. In addition, it is much easier for a large corporation to negotiate favorable discounts from suppliers because of the larger orders and possibly easier delivery conditions or other benefits not available to small business.

I once knew an older man, operating as a small business consultant (and doing a wonderful job, by the way). He had worked for many years as comptroller of a regional department store chain. His credo was "Son, always remember, it's a sight easier to buy a profit than it is to sell one." The suppliers' reps that came to see him hated the man but his clients certainly loved him

The small businessman is penalized in many other ways, also. Since he is self-employed he has to pay the matching portion of his social security tax and the matching portion of his Medicare payment. This is all based on his profit shown on Schedule C. It is very regressive and, depending on his age, can boost his effective tax rate to as much as 80% on the top portion of his income. Sometimes it is better to work for less money as long as you are working for someone else.

Interestingly enough, though, sometimes the tax laws benefit some of the small businessmen, especially when they also benefit big business. Some years ago, life insurance companies were not able to help their agents be covered by retirement plans because the agents were and always had been, treated as self-employed people so they didn't qualify for company pension plans or 401(k) plans. So, some bright legislator created a new kind of employee called the "statutory employee". At the employers' option, all that was required was a simple check mark on the sales person's W-2 form and that person would be able to use a Schedule C to report his income and expenses rather than the old Form 2106, which was a favorite audit signal for the IRS. Also, even though filing a Schedule C, the statutory employee could also be covered under company plan(s) or 401(k).

This neat little arrangement helped the insurance companies do a good thing for their sales personnel and at the same time did a tremendously better thing for the sales personnel who were being treated as small business operators. They could have the best of both worlds.

After the establishment of the "statutory employee" designation for, basically, life insurance sales people many other outside sales people qualified for the designation. It is one instance where the small businessman has scored a small victory over the stifling bonds of the income tax laws.

The almost overpowering burden of the record-keeping required of the small businessman takes an inordinate amount of the businessperson's time and energy, to say nothing of the financial cost. And, even if every effort is made to be within the rules, one never is altogether certain that the IRS won't come knocking on the door.

Another sometimes frustrating problem for small business comes more under the heading of payroll tax than income tax and that is workman's compensation insurance. This can result in rather harsh consequences if the records are not properly handled and the audits are, like in use tax audits, very detailed and the auditors are more than usually picky. The rates of tax (or premiums) are staggering in some categories of employment and, again, as in the income tax field, we get into a definition problem. What you see isn't necessarily what you get.

The UTT tax probably would not be applicable to the workman's comp insurance since it is a constantly changing "tax" subject to changes in medical costs and other factors such as compensatory damage claims and legal liability claims.

In summary, the UTT tax would be a blessing for small business, not only in the reduction of tax but relief from the ever-present dread of that odious letter from the IRS, "Dear Taxpayer……."

President Bush recently stated that the present Tax Code's complexity is costing the nation over $300-billion each year just to keep records, file returns, etc. If we took this burden off our business world, especially the small-business portion, think about how nice it would be.

If you add to the $300-billion above the estimated $350-billion that people do not pay, ignore or avoid it comes very nearly three quarters of a billion dollars. The proposed budget this year is something like 2.7-trillion dollars so with the UTT tax we could, in theory, reduces the Federal budget by over 20%.

Chapter Fourteen

Politically Out of Date

The decade of the '20's in the last century must have really been a riotous time. It was the age of the flapper girls, Bye, Bye, Blackbird, boom and bust stock market bubbles, prohibition, and the early automobile. Then came the inevitable downside, Black Friday and the Great Depression.

I was born too late to see the '20's but I saw more than I wanted to see of the '30's. I was not born in a log cabin but I was moved into one when I was about six weeks old and lived in it until my late teens. The land around the cabin had been cleared by my grandfather in the early 1900's and part of the cabin complex had been built by him.

Grandpa John was a Socialist (with a capital "S", I was told)) and I remember him talking animatedly in the 30's as I was growing up about his theory that the government should give everybody a pension when they were older. I don't remember the details of his plan but I know that the state of Oklahoma did work out some sort of "Old Age Pension" plan and Grandpa was very appreciative of his monthly check. It kept him from working in his old age. Oklahoma in those years was a very wealthy state compared to most because it was an oil producing state. I suppose that was where the pension money came from but in Grandpa's Socialistic agenda it probably was taken from the rich and given to the poor.

The Socialist concept was running rampant in the aftermath of World War I. Trotsky and Lenin were the movers and shakers at first and caught the attention of many of the workers of America with their ideas of re-distribution of wealth and communization of property. Their idea, though, of the state owning everything, didn't set too well with the American workers. They had had a history of private ownership of property and didn't want to go completely too full communism. And, at that point, as best I have been able to tell, some very. very politically bright people moved in, took over the Democrat party and picked out a diabolically conceived title for their so-called but controlling wing of the Democrat party, that title being the Liberals. They are not, and never have been "liberal" even though their title might suggest they are. The word suggests philanthropic, benign, benevolent, tolerant, nice folk and the like. Far from it! They have controlled the Democrat party for seventy-five years.

In the very last few years the Liberal/Socialists have lost many battles and most of the elections. Speaker Newt Gingrich and his Contract with America in the early '90's began a real trend of refutation of the strident Liberal calls for more and more "pie-in-the-sky" programs to be paid for by re-distribution of the wealth schemes.

It is easy to see how the Liberals seized control of the Democrat party. The economic turmoil of the '30's caused a lot of damage to the American dream that had survived a recent turbulent century which had encapsulated three foreign wars and a civil war. They merely had to have some public speakers that could make grandiose promises and they had the votes in hand. A hungry man with a family at home will grasp at any proposed solution sometimes. And so, the old 'free lunch' 'pie-in-the-sky" promises held the controlling hand for almost seventy-five years.

The graduated income tax is almost the last bastion of defense for the Liberals. It is the Robin Hood defense that has been the theme song for them. Rob from the rich" sounds good but whether it is good or not depends, like the graduated income tax itself, on the definition of who is rich. Someone once said, "There are two kinds of people in this world, the sane and the insane. And the sane ones do the classifying."

It has always been astonishing to me how leading Liberals argue stringently for the graduated income tax and the "death" tax fiasco and yet the Kennedy family fortune along with many others continues to proliferate through thick and thin and all the progeny keep singing the same old "soak the rich" and "re-distribute the wealth" schemes.

The UTT tax plan is primarily one of spreading the tax base and taking the terrible pressure off the middle class and small businessmen. It is a fair tax in that it carries the same rate for all. It has some of the features of a VAT tax and some of the features of a sales tax but by broadening the tax base to such as extent that it does it has little, if any, or the regressive qualities of either. It has very little of the social control factors drooled over by the Liberals and very little invasion of privacy concern. It is easy to collect, almost effortless to transmit to the U.S. Treasury.

There will be protests from many people about the Federal government collecting taxes for the states, I am sure. Most of these will be initiated by state employees whose jobs would be obliterated. There will be strident and vociferous speeches and protests from the Liberals, of course. Actually, if they were, or had been, smart, they would have changed the graduated income tax some years ago to some sort of consumer tax or at least devised some method of expanding the tax base for an income tax at a much lower rate. Their very existence, however, is threatened, however, by any loss of social control and social control cannot succeed in a consumer tax program.

Adoption of the UTT tax will depend on the voters or America. The plan will need a "champion"who will take charge of the idea and take it to the American people. He (or she) will, I think, be a shoo-in for President. Who, among the voting populace is going to resist a candidate who says, "Forget the 1040 form forever. Pay your paltry tax at the cash register. Never worry about the IRS again."

It will be interesting to see what kind of plan the Liberals will present to counteract the UTT tax. What kind of spin will they have to put on their plans in order to keep their social control agenda? And what will they have left for a platform?

Chapter Fifteen

Frequently Asked Questions (FAQ's)

In the following pages I will try to answer some of the most interesting questions that have been asked about the UTT tax plan.

Q. What will happen to my IRA's and my 401K?

A. Nothing but good things. Your savings will still be there, possibly with fewer restrictions on withdrawals. Actually, you might even use the savings plan already started as a base for a long-term savings program with the extra take-home pay you would have with the UTT tax plan. A national savings plan could be sponsored that would enhance the benefits of the social security program. All economists will agree that the solidity of a country's economy is a vigorous savings base by its citizens. What better way to save since we have IRA's and 401K's already at hand?

Q. What would be the result if I sold a family heirloom on e-Bay for, Say, $30,000.00? To someone in India? Would *the person have to pay the UTT tax? And, if I am not normally a commercial account holder, would I have to open a special account so the bank would hold out the tax?*

A. I would think that the buyer would have to pay the tax. That will be up to the Congress to spell out specific rules but it would seem that that would be a taxable transaction. As to depositing the tax collected that could be handled in a number of different ways. You could be required to pay it directly to the U.S. Treasury account at your bank or personal account deposit slips could have a box on their face that could account for unusual deposits by personal account holders. Of course, if you were an antique dealer it would be taken care of in the usual manner. Also, it might be possible that e-Bay would withhold and deposit the tax.

This said, we might think for a minute about payment of the tax by a foreign person or organization. Why not? We have developed a tremendous market and should be repaid for the development that individuals and organizations have created over the last century. In the countries with the VAT tax you must pay the tax and then apply for a refund later (but only if you apply for over a certain minimum amount of refund. I was in London in the mid-90's, however, and applied for almost $95.00 in refunds and never heard a word.

Another factor might be mentioned here, also, and that is the problem of just plain cheating in this case. If we assume that the UTT tax would be, say, 1%, the selling party would have a check or draft or some other instrument representing money. He might just cash the check and hide the whole stack of hundred-dollar bills under his mattress. Or, there might be a regulation in the UTT tax code that says that if something likes this happens and he is trying to cheat for more then $250.00 he could face a $10,000.00 fine or a trip to the slammer. Who would risk that for a mere $250.00?

Q. *I am a farmer. Would I have to collect the UTT tax from hay buyers or livestock buyers? And what about all the unused depreciation tied up in the expensive equipment I have?*

A. Yes, you would collect the UTT tax. You would be classified as a Commercial enterprise and would collect the tax just the same as if you were a grocer or a landlord. And, in answer to your question of depreciation you would lose any tax advantage still locked into your investment in equipment. However, you would gain from the standpoint of paying out income taxes, sometimes on crops unsold. And think of the many, many hours you would save from having to do less arduous paperwork.

Q. *What will happen to charitable organizations if the income tax code isn't there to push donors to support them?*

A. The bulk of the non-taxable organizations and foundations will Survive the changeover. However, many of the fly-by-night groups and foundations will fall by the wayside. It has been shown over the years that many of them are operated only for a few paychecks for management. Contributors will have more money to contribute under the UTT tax so the well-organized and well-attended churches, foundations and other charitable entities will go on as usual. There is one thing that should be noted here, however, and that is that the charitable organizations will pay the tax when they buy supplies, land, automobiles, trucks, salaries, etc. I suppose the Treasury could excuse them from paying the tax when they buy something but in the interest of making less paperwork and keeping a level playing field with no exemptions, no deductions, no favoritism they should pay the tax.

There has always been a question in my mind as to why the U.S. Treasury has to make the decision as to whether a certain organization is qualified to be classified as a "non-profit" organization and exempt from tax laws. Isn't this a bit outside the limits of responsibility for the tax collecting arm of the government? The U.S. Treasury should be devoted to collecting taxes, not defining the social or moral values of organizations.

Q. About 15 months ago I bought a tremendous home on a PGA-rated golf course that had just opened. The land and home values have sky-rocketed since I bought and I now have an offer in which I would realize a profit of over $300,000.00. What would be my tax under the present tax code and what would it be under the UTT tax code?

A. I would estimate your tax under the present code at about $42-45 Thousand dollars. Under the UTT tax system you would pay no tax at all at the time of sale. You would have paid your 1% on the purchase price when you bought it 15 months ago. Under the present system you would be able to pay no tax at all at either purchase or sale if you had occupied the home for two years before the sale.

Q Would I still have social security and Medicare payments deducted from my paycheck?

A. Yes, I'm afraid so, at least for some period of time until all the bugs are worked out of the system. After a few years I think that legislators will find that by broadening the tax base to the ultimate, as they will have done with the UTT tax, budgetary problems are easily solved. I doubt that Congress would immediately give up the social security or Medicare Entitlements, especially with their ever-rising costs. After a period of time to find our boundaries, we should expect to see payroll taxes either greatly reduced or gone altogether. Then we should take the terrible burden off the backs of our grand-children and great-grand-children, that of keeping us in our dotage. The young people of today have little confidence in the present system. All the present system needs is money and the UTT tax can produce that.

Q. You have a good idea here, my friend, but it will never happen. You would never get this through Congress in the first place and the states would never let the Federal government collect their taxes for them. You're wasting your time. It'll just never happen!

A. This comment came from one of my hard-nosed clients who has had many tax problems over the many years of our friendship. I have tried to explain to him many times that the UTT tax is a tax that relieves the middle-class of the terrible responsibility of providing almost all the revenue the Federal government requires. I believe that a poll of all voters asking about the UTT tax system would show that about 75% would vote for its support. The other 25% would be Liberal/Socialists who would resent any effort to free people of their social control programs that have been imbedded in our decaying graduated tax system.

Q. This is nothing but a giveaway for the rich and the big corporations. It does nothing for the working man and the middle-class. The rich ought to be taxed at about 50% and the big corporations about the same. The poor should be paying not tax at all. Your plan is pure Rich Republican. It will never work!

A. It was unfortunate that this Liberal/Socialist remark was made by an acquaintance and one-time client. It only shows that he was parroting the standard line of the Far Left. The UTT tax does cut taxes for the rich, it does cut taxes for the large corporations but it also almost completely cuts taxes for the middle class and the poor. However, the good thing it does far out-weighs the supposed bad things. It restores initiative into our younger generation workers, it puts money back into the pockets of the families of our country so that they can raise their quality of life, it gets the IRS out of our private financial affairs, and it gets everyone back into the act of being a citizen, not just a name and number on a 1040 form.

Q. Why are you so sure that the states will agree to let the U. S. Treasury collect their taxes? They could just go it alone with their own tax systems, couldn't they?

A Yes, they certainly could but at a tremendous cost. Most of the states that have an income tax merely use the Federal adjusted gross income figures to start their tax-collecting process and have little in their state tax code except (many) little extras that give back certain credits and add little tax amounts to it's taxpayers. It will be somewhat disconcerting, I would think, when a state keeps on with the old programs when it could piggyback with the Federal and cut tremendous costs from its tax-collecting costs. Or, they might be given the option to make their own arrangements within their borders and have their collections paid directly to them by the collecting banks.

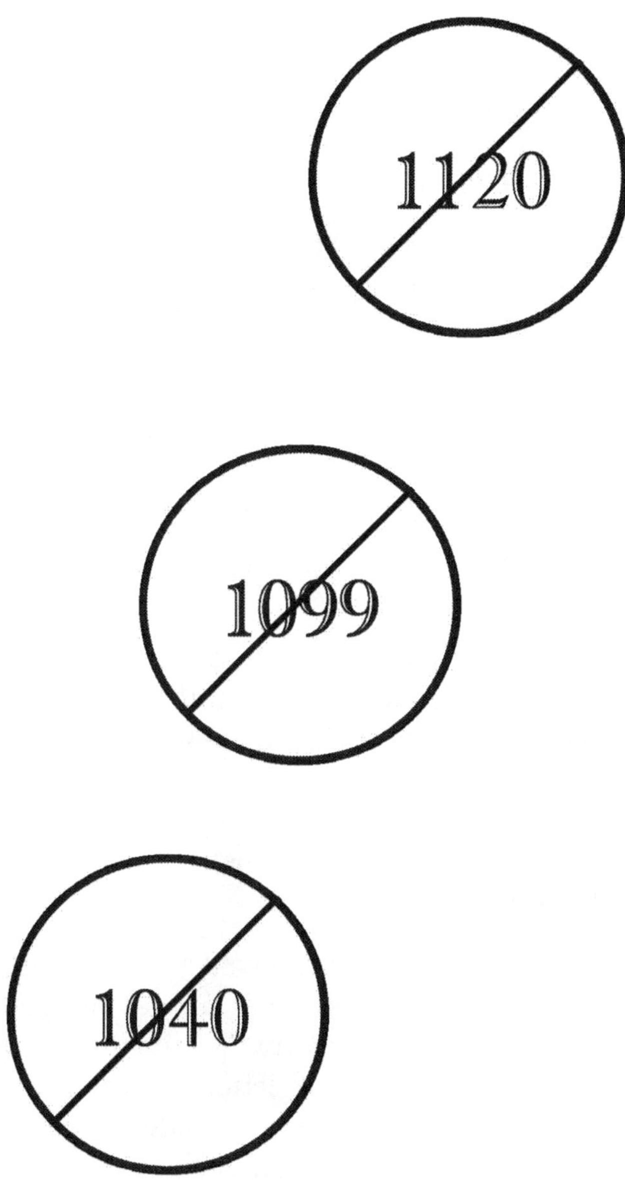

Chapter Sixteen

From the Beginning

The plan for the UTT tax was born after a particularly arduous tax season in the summer of 1992. My brother Gene and I worked on details of collection of the tax, problems involving estimation of national taxable cash flow and dozens of other items.

A number of other problems, personal and business, intervened and little action were taken until late in 1995 and the Gingrich group's Contract with America had taken effect. Then the subject of change in our outdated tax system became a hot topic for awhile. Steve Forbes pushed his "flat tax" idea; others tried to rally support for a national sales tax at a rate that was astronomical.

At about that time we received a letter from Bill Archer which validated our original ideas almost perfectly. This letter is reproduced as the final exhibit of this book. The UTT tax design is almost to the letter the type of tax advocated by Congressman Archer, adding only a means of collection that was purely twenty-first century vintage.

As we said in the opening pages of this book, the UTT tax could not have worked at all thirty years ago but makes perfect sense today. With the explosive growth of computer technology the tax collection feature of the UTT tax plan makes it all possible. The system would be so easy to install it would be almost seamless in the changeover. The details would be understandable by the taxpayers and there should be few errors made in either collection or depositing of the tax.

It has been a long road to this point but we think the UTT tax system is the only workable alternative we have seen and would create a fair and consistent tax system that would relieve the nation's taxpayers of at least one problem they all face, the annual headache of filing tax returns.

Exhibit One

Dim Outlook for Alternatives

On October 19, 1992, I wrote the following letter to the editor of the local newspaper:

Editor
Times News
Twin Falls, Idaho

In all the furor of the election campaign, we hear all kinds of proposals to raise taxes, primarily income and payroll taxes. I think we have some very sophisticated politicians around that do not realize that we are scraping the bottom of the barrel insofar as increasing the yield from income and payroll taxes. It just isn't there to harvest from small businesses, farmers and wage earners.

A national sales tax has been talked about for years and several foreign countries have experimented with this idea for the last decade or so. They call theirs a value added tax or a VAT and if you want to see some terrible examples of small business problems just go to England and buy something. Prices will astound you.

No one has proposed a transaction tax, however. This tax would apply to every "transaction" made in our country. The "purchaser" or recipient or services or any transaction would pay a 1% tax upon making the transaction. The only persons exempt from paying the tax would be U.S. and state governments.

The transaction tax would be collected by the banks through the deposits. Every deposit slip would have two sections on it, one for the regular deposit and one for the transaction tax collected.

As an indication of what might be expected from such a tax, I totaled the dollar value 15 most active stocks on the New York Stock Exchange for October 15, 1992. The transaction tax that would have amounted, even on this small portion of the securities alone, to almost 27 million dollars!

There would be no hidey-hole corners for the rich or the poor, the anointed political aristocracy, no one. This tax would be the only way we would be able to tax the oil sheiks, foreign investors, gambling casinos and many of the funds now going out of the country to escape the loophole-ridden income tax regulations.

The income tax law is a law of definition. I think it is time to set up some laws that are fair to all but with a lowest-common-denominator definition. The social-control politicians would say this tax would not offer much relief, and would fight it to the bitter end.

Collection of such a tax would have been impossible even 10 years ago but now, with the computer networks we have, the Treasury wouldn't have to wait for months to use the cash collections. They would have them almost daily.

Sincerely,
D.D. Lawley
Certified Public Accountant

This letter was never published because it was too long for the editor's needs, was supposedly too technical and had to understand. I didn't argue with the editor. It was his newspaper, not mine. However, the idea was there then and none of the conditions have changed. Since then we have had proposals made by ordinarily sensible men for things like the "flat tax" on income or "flat tax" sales tax. Both ideas were resounding "flops" in the public's eyes. It's hard to tell anyone who is buying a $25,000.00 automobile that they will also owe 17% of that figure, or $4,250.00 for sales tax. They had to arrive at that figure by giving away so many exemptions and donations that only a few people would be paying taxes.

The "flat tax' is just a rehash of the same old box of bad news that we already have. You might be able to file your return on a postcard but all the other problems are still there, big time. This system is still taxation by definition and embodies all the same problems we now have. We must broaden the tax base so the middle class is not taxed out of existence.

It must be noted that all the figures and ideas displayed in this chapter were quoted from records from 1992, some 12 years ago. The transaction tax was quoted at 1% in the charts shown. At the time, we had no way of calculating the total transactions for the entire country and still don't. But some reasonable estimates could be made. Perhaps it might take a 2% tax or even a 3%. Who knows? At any rate it would be far less than we are paying now through the graduated income tax and would fairly distribute the burden of tax to "where the money is", as the saying goes.

(Note: This was a magazine article written circa 1995 but never published. It was submitted to at least two magazines but was not accepted by either.)

Exhibit Two

United States Senate

(June 2, 1993)

Duard Lawley
PO Box 962
Twin Falls, ID 83301

Dear Duard:

Thank you for your letter about our current tax system. I appreciate having the benefit of your thoughts.

The development of a tax system that treats all taxpayers fairly has been one of my most important objectives in Congress. Our current system of progressive taxation has become an instrument for social change through tax incentives, deductions and exemptions rather than a system to raise revenue to fund the Federal Government.

Over the years, I have supported a 10 percent flat tax rate. Such a tax would be much simpler in its application and would erase the bias that our current progressive tax system has against success and providing for one's family. You can be assured I will keep your comments in mind.

Unfortunately, hundreds of interest groups and individuals who have enjoyed the benefits of special tax privileges argue for their continuation. Many of these provisions may be good for the economy, providing incentives for a higher standard of living and promoting continued economic growth. Unfortunately, many aren't so helpful. The challenge will be to simplify taxes quickly, effectively, and equitably.

The concept of a national sales tax has both positives and negatives. It is positive in that a tax on spending does encourage productivity and savings – both of which are good for our economy. It is negative in that it is the most regressive form of tax, because it has a disproportionate impact on those with lower income. Additionally, the sales tax is one of the last revenue measures available to the states that have not been invaded by federal government. If there were to be a national sales tax enacted, then it should be accompanied by corresponding elimination of federal income tax. This is simply not likely to happen.

I have always been opposed to a VAT system because it imposes a tax at each stage of processing a product: production, distribution, wholesale, and retail levels, not to mention a few more for some products. It's like a sales tax, but collected at every step at which the value of the original product is increased or added to. The more you can hide a tax from the taxpayer, the easier it is to raise taxes. Enacting a VAT creates the possibility of runaway taxation by the federal government.

Again, thank you for contacting me. If I may be of further help, please let me know.

Sincerely,

Larry E. Craig
U.S. Senator

LEC/amm

Exhibit Three

Further Ideas on the Transaction Tax

Since the original idea of the transaction tax was promoted (April 1992) we have had a major campaign and election and a subsequent inauguration. We have a new President who has vowed to "clean up our domestic economy," take some of the tax burden off the "middle class" and other assorted goodies. Good Luck, Bill!

We are even closer to the bottom of the barrel in tax revenues than we were a year ago, the IRS audited their even-smaller percentage of returns last year, the list of taxpayers who owe the government billions of dollars in uncollected (and uncollectible) taxes grew even more and no one who has any voice has come forward with any logical solution to the mess. Oh, there are a couple of proposals for a national sales tax, but a sales tax, as such, is a regressive tax that would be nothing but a burden on lower and middle income taxpayers.

The value of a transaction tax would (or could be) threefold: (1) It would eliminate taxation by definition, e.g. the Tax Code, (2) It would tax the <u>flow</u> of money rather than the profit derived from that flow, and (3) Layer after layer of tax collection functionaries could be eliminated from the present process. Another ancillary benefit would accrue to the banks if they were paid, say, 5% of their collections in return for their labor expended and use of their tremendously expensive computer systems they have developed over the last decade.

In addition, the cash would start flowing to the Treasury within two days after the law went into effect, not 3 months to 18 months later.

We would then have the latitude to greatly simplify the income tax laws. No deductions, no exemptions and a flat 10% tax on all income of any kind over $20,000.00. Or, if in doubt, put a phase-down or –out percentage on the income tax over the next 10 years. Or, give a flat credit on all income tax returns of 1% of the gross income shown on that return.

It would be, I think, surprising to the Treasury how much income would be realized from foreign interests. Oh, the exporters would hate the idea, I am sure. If Russia wanted to buy a billion dollars worth of wheat I'm sure that they wouldn't relish the payment of a 1% tax in addition to the price. But, after all, we have set up an infrastructure (at taxpayer expense, yet) to spawn "transactions" both domestic worldwide. Why shouldn't those people help pay for it, also? As it is, Japanese industrialists can come to the U.S., buy a world famous golf course for some astronomical figure of $95 million, adjust it so that it makes no "profit" and pay no tax at all except for local and/or state property taxes.

This transaction tax, with no exemptions, remember, would increase the cost of goods slightly, also. A household washer and dryer, for example, would increase in cost by probably $25.00 for a set. An automobile's cost would increase. Aunt Millie's prescription at the drug store would increase, also, but the tax would be her contribution to a well-funded Medicare program that would not be in danger of collapse next year or the year after.

The American taxpayers are at the end of the rope. They need a champion!

Duard Lawley
Certified Public Accountant
Twin Falls, Idaho
January 25, 1993

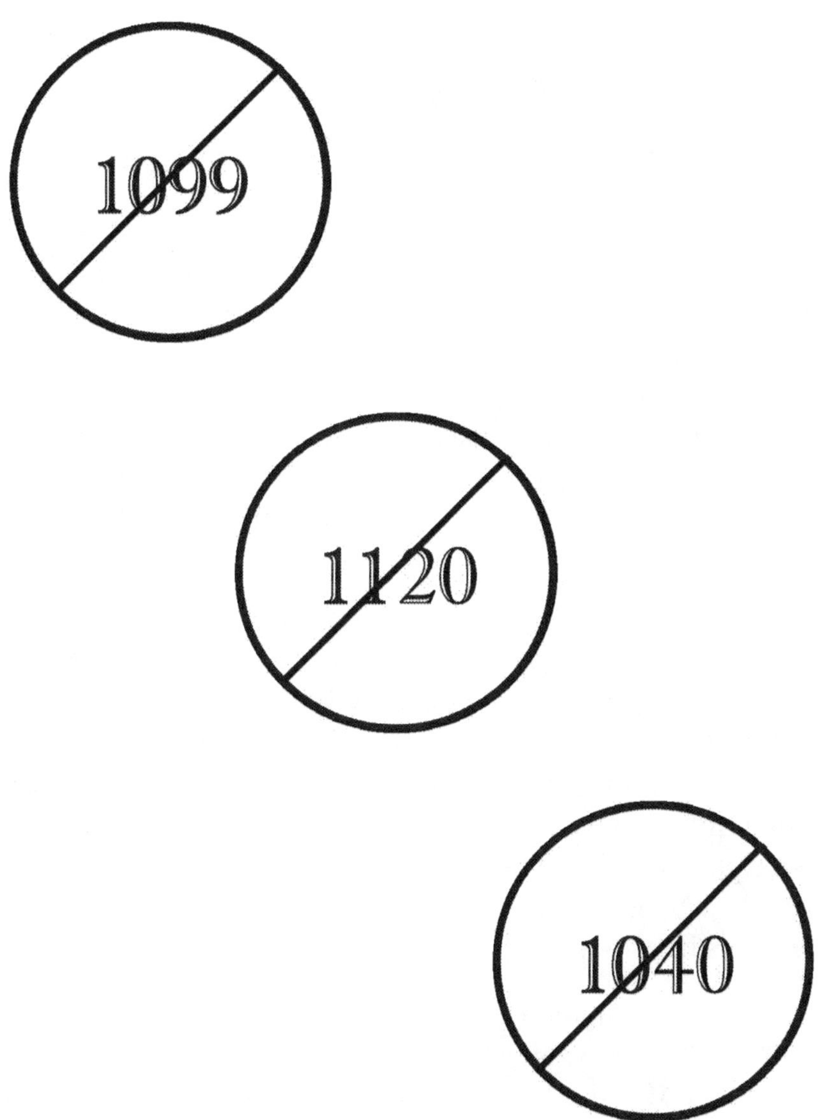

Exhibit Four

The Wicked Witch is Dead...

I am speaking, of course, of our old nemesis, the income tax system. Born in a socialistic era, patched, re-patched, remodeled, the old girl has almost made her last gasp. The latest public outcry has resulted in more patchwork laws, rules and regulations. The apologists for the system say the IRS is going to become more user-friendly, etc. Sound familiar? Same string, different yo-yo. We've heard it all before.

The income tax is an idea preying on some of the basest emotions in human nature, those of envy, jealousy and greed. It creates class discrimination and is obviously at odds with the American dream of private enterprise and individual freedom. It is a code of law that initially was promoted to tax the rich but has turned into one that taxes the dwindling middle class and even the poor. You might believe the liberal politicians when they say that the poor pay no income taxes but you would be wrong. The poor pay higher prices for everything they buy because of income taxes. They are paying income tax, they just don't know it.

The tax code is one of definition. As we accountants and tax lawyers all know, all you have to do to lower the income tax of a client is to find a small point of definition that will enable the client to slip into a little niche of partial or non-taxability of just some of his income. These points can be found (sometimes quite easily) by winnowing through the thousands of tax cases that have been decided over the last seventy-five or so years since the tax code became a major influence on our lives. The client might never be questioned on the definition, either, since the IRS audits a smaller percentage of returns each year.

Another enforcement problem for the IRS has not really been talked about by the media or the politicians. It is so new and yet so mind-boggling that the average person cannot imagine the consequences.

This method of avoiding taxes is only for the greedy and/or the unlawful at the moment but potentially, I believe, carries a momentous threat to our national financial well-being. This problem arises from technology and lies in the ability to do business in cyberspace, if a business or individual chooses to do so. Sell something over the Internet, have the funds deposited to a Swiss or other secret bank account, transfer them back to the U.S. by some arcane method, deal in cash, etc. You get the picture. Many people who might be on the borderline of honesty would be forced to go along with the scheme out of sheer financial self-defense. Meanwhile, the IRS is decades behind in computer technology that could possibly catch such a tax fraud. They are also woefully short of personnel who are computer-smart and have a very short budget with which to work, anyhow.

Another point seldom, if ever, mentioned by the politicians and media, is the loss of tax revenue from foreign interests. We have created a financial edifice in the United States that is the last safe resort for investment in the world. All countries, even our enemies, buy our investments whether those investments are shares of stock, bonds, commodities, or whatever. Any profits they take on these investments are seldom, if ever, taxed. Multi-national corporations commonly sidestep our tax laws by operating policies that use off-shore residency or tax breaks to avoid paying income tax. We have innumerable tax treaties with almost every country in the world and these treaties have tremendous loopholes that very effectively stifle any attempt to collect a fair tax from foreign interests.

What, then, are we going to do? The only two alternatives mentioned so far are the flat tax and some sort of consumer tax, i.e., retail sales tax. The flat tax is almost impossible to understand and would only be another redo of the income tax that we have. You might be able to file a return on a postcard, but the data required behind the return would be as great, or greater, than today's system. Also, the rates mentioned so far would not provide nearly enough revenue for our needs. Our army of bureaucrats would never stand for that!

The retail sales tax would not be a viable option because the best opinions I have heard yet are that the rage would have to be 15% or more to meet our financial requirements for government. Every state in the union that has a sales tax will tell you that a sales tax is terribly hard to administer what with all the exempt sales, out-of-state sales, catalog sales, etc. This would be magnified for Federal sales tax. We would have a veritable army of IRS personnel issuing exemption cards to the millions of people and organizations demanding them. If you are talking about a rate of 15% it would be hard for anyone to stomach the $2,000.00 or so in sales tax on a new car. And, assuming no exemption, how about the farmer buying a new tractor? He could end up paying $5,000.00 or more in nothing but the sales tax.

Aside from all these, the sales tax would create tremendous quantities of paperwork and horrendous liabilities for business. Basically, the business collecting a sales tax that has numerous exemptions has a situation forced on them that makes them potentially liable if they do not correctly enforce the tax laws. It almost seems as though the taxing authorities believe that businesses have nothing else to worry about except being correctly in step with the tax law in question. A sales tax, in its usual format, is potentially far more fraught with liability than even an income tax. The person or organization at the collection point tends to become an unwilling agent for government and would not have the same shields from liability that the government employee would enjoy by being an employee.

The only answer to our problem would be a tax on cash flow. This actually translates into a "transaction" tax. The person who pays the money in any transaction actually pays the tax.

The tax rate of a transaction tax would be 1% and there would be no exemptions, no deductions, no forms to be filed by any of the payers of the tax. The government would get its money within 10 business days. The IRS would consist of a battery of computers that could very easily ferret out any one who didn't deposit the government's tax receipts within 10 days of such receipt.

This would be the fairest of all taxes in that everyone would pay the same rate, and the rate would be so small that there would be little incentive to cheat. True, the poor family with family income of, say, $15,000.00 might pay $150.00 per year, but on the other hand the rich would pay tax of 1%, also, and on amounts sometimes running into the millions.

Now, the financial markets would provide the largest percentage of all the tax collected. Estimates of the tax collections form financial markets alone run to $3-1/2 trillion. Add in another $750 billion to $1-1/2 trillion from domestic collections and we are looking at a possible $4 trillion dollars. This amount would void the need for any other taxes such as estate and excise taxes. It would probably pay the social security taxes for most people, provide funds to the states to cut the need for state income taxes, and provide funds to retire the national debt over a reasonable period of time.

Technically, the tax would be easier to collect than a retail sales tax since all transactions would be taxable and no hard decisions would have to be made by people who would not be capable of making them. The only form that would be required would be a deposit slip and even that would be only a small blank box on the collector's regular deposit slip. The bank's computer would carry the government's portion of the deposit to the U.S. Treasury's account (every bank would have such an account). Then, within a certain period of time the bank would transfer the account balance directly to the U.S Treasury. No forms, no paperwork, no returns.

This method of collection is already being done and has been done for years in regard to payroll taxes. The transaction tax would only be done on a larger scale. The banks should be paid something, also, for their activities on behalf of the government. The banking computer system in America is the best in the world and would relieve the government of a tremendous cost in computer systems within the very near future. Estimates of the cost of the required computer system runs into the billions of dollars and would take years to put into place. If the transaction tax were implemented it could be done in a matter of months.

The transaction tax would affect every individual, every business, every element of our society and our country. It would be fair, easy to collect, and would make the present army of tax collectors obsolete. Those who regard the income tax as a method of social control would object strenuously, I am sure, but something must be done soon or we will have no society to control.

BILL ARCHER
7TH DISTRICT, TEXAS

CHAIRMAN
WAYS AND MEANS
COMMITTEE

JOINT COMMITTEE
ON TAXATION

Congress of the United States
House of Representatives

WASHINGTON OFFICE:
1236 LONGWORTH
HOUSE OFFICE BUILDING
WASHINGTON, DC 20515-4307
(202) 225-2571
FAX (202) 225-4381

DISTRICT OFFICE:
10000 MEMORIAL DRIVE, SUITE 620
HOUSTON, TX 77024-3490
(713) 682-8828
FAX (713) 680-8070

December 15, 1995

Mr. Gene D. Lawley
276 Blue Lakes Boulevard, North
Twin Falls, Idaho 83301

Dear Gene:

Thank you very much for your recent letter.

I'm glad to know of your support for a consumption tax. As Chairman of the Ways and Means Committee, I held hearings on June 6-8 to consider eliminating our current income tax and replacing it with some type of consumption tax. I'm about convinced that we can't effectively make the income tax the tool that the American people will be most comfortable with and the engine that will drive job creation, economic activity and increase the family income for the people of this country. I want to emphasize, however, that any consumption tax would be a complete alternative to the income tax, not an add-on tax.

There are many positive aspects to changing our basic tax structure. First, it would greatly simplify the way we pay taxes and would remove the IRS from people's lives as much as possible. Individuals currently spend about $65 billion annually to complete their returns. It is estimated that the total time spent annually preparing taxes is over 1.8 billion hours for individual taxpayers and 3.6 billion hours for businesses. The U.S. tax law is quickly approaching one million words in length and federal tax regulations are already over five million words. Add to this the $14 billion it takes to administer the tax law and the costs surrounding our current income tax become more and more evident.

Taxing consumption rather than income would encourage savings and investment. Our domestic savings rate has declined in recent years, falling from $247.9 billion in 1992 to $192.6 billion in 1993. Thus, less saving was available to finance American investment and, as a consequence, U.S. imports of foreign capital increased. The increased savings and investment that would come from such a plan would increase the capital available and spur economic growth. A Cato Institute study predicted that a national sales tax would more than triple the nation's savings rate, from 2.5 percent to 7.6 percent. In addition, it would increase America's international competitiveness. U.S. exports would not be taxed and imports would be subject to the same broad-based consumption tax as U.S. goods.

A broad-based consumption tax would allow the federal government to finally collect taxes from the underground economy. The U.S. Treasury Department estimates that it is unable to collect $125

Mr. Gene D. Lawley
December 15, 1995
Page 2

billion in income taxes every year. I personally believe that this is a low estimate and the real number could be as high as $300 to $400 billion. Currently, we force law-abiding taxpayers to carry the tax burden for those who have dropped out of the system and don't pay income taxes. While it is uncommon for drug dealers to file federal income taxes, it is not uncommon for drug dealers to purchase clothes, stereos or anything else subject to a consumption tax.

Criticism has been leveled at taxing consumption rather than income. In particular, those opposed to the consumption tax state that it would be regressive and hidden. However, I would like to point out that a consumption-based tax has supporters from both conservative and liberal thinkers. The argument is raised that it is a regressive tax because the poor consume a much greater percentage of their income and would, thus, pay a higher percentage of their income. However, regressivity could be addressed by rebating a basic level of consumption. Rebating, and at what level to rebate will certainly be part of the consumption tax debate. It is also argued that it is a hidden tax. Maybe, but through withholding taxes, our current income tax is largely hidden and the pain of paying taxes is dispersed throughout the year. While I admit there are obstacles to eliminating the income tax and replacing it, I believe the time has come to look at a tax that is simple, fair, pro-growth and pro-jobs.

With best regards,

Sincerely,

Bill Archer
Member of Congress

BA/grb

LARRY E. CRAIG
IDAHO

HART SENATE OFFICE BUILDING
(202) 224-2752

AGRICULTURE, NUTRITION, AND FORESTRY
ENERGY AND NATURAL RESOURCES
SPECIAL COMMITTEE ON AGING

United States Senate

WASHINGTON, DC 20510-1203

June 2, 1993

Duard Lawley
PO Box 962
Twin Falls, ID 83301

Dear Duard:

Thank you for your letter about our current tax system. I appreciate having the benefit of your thoughts.

The development of a tax system that treats all taxpayers fairly has been one of my most important objectives in Congress. Our current system of progressive taxation has become an instrument for social change through tax incentives, deductions and exemptions rather than a system to raise revenue to fund the Federal government.

Over the years, I have supported a 10 percent flat tax rate. Such a tax would be much simpler in its application and would erase the bias that our current progressive tax system has against success and providing for one's family. You can be assured I will keep your comments in mind.

Unfortunately, hundreds of interest groups and individuals who have enjoyed the benefits of special tax privileges argue for their continuation. Many of these provisions may be good for the economy, providing incentives for a higher standard of living and promoting continued economic growth. Unfortunately, many aren't so helpful. The challenge will be to simplify taxes quickly, effectively, and equitably.

The concept of a national sales tax has both positives and negatives. It is positive in that a tax on spending does encourage productivity and savings -- both of which are good for our economy. It is negative in that it is the most regressive form of tax, because it has a disproportionate impact on those with lower income. Additionally, the sales tax is one of the last revenue measures available to the states that has not been invaded by the federal government. If there were to be a national sales tax enacted, then it should be accompanied by corresponding elimination of federal income tax. This is simply not likely to happen.

I have always been opposed to a VAT system because it imposes a tax at each stage of processing a product: production, distribution, wholesale, and retail levels, not to mention a few more for some products. It's like a sales tax, but collected at every step at which the value of the original product is

RESOURCE CENTER 304 NORTH 8TH STREET ROOM 147 BOISE, IDAHO 83702 | 304 NORTH 8TH STREET ROOM 149 BOISE, IDAHO 83702 | 103 NORTH 4TH STREET COEUR D'ALENE, IDAHO 83814 | 633 MAIN STREET LEWISTON, IDAHO 83501 | 250 SOUTH 4TH AVENUE POCATELLO, IDAHO 83201 | 1292 ADDISON AVENUE EAST TWIN FALLS, IDAHO 83301 | 2539 CHANNING WAY IDAHO FALLS, IDAHO 83404 increased or added to. The more you can hide a tax from the taxpayer, the easier it is to raise taxes. Enacting a VAT creates the possibility of runaway taxation by the federal government.

Again, thank you for contacting me. If I may be of further help, please let me know.

Sincerely,

LARRY E. CRAIG
U.S. Senator

LEC\amm

1040

1120

1099

www.ingramcontent.com/pod-product-compliance
Lightning Source LLC
Chambersburg PA
CBHW022119170526
45157CB00004B/1697

* 9 7 8 1 4 2 0 8 8 3 1 2 1 *